RECORDED VERSIONS
GUITAR

AUTHENTIC TRANSCRIPTIONS
WITH NOTES AND TABLATURE

THE FOLK-ROCK GUITAR COLLECTION

P9-DVG-638

ISBN 0-7935-8125-7

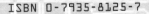

HAL•LEONARD® CORPORATION

7777 W. BLUEMOUND RD. P.O. BOX 13819 MILWAUKEE, WI 53213

Visit Hal Leonard Online at
www.halleonard.com

American Pie

Words and Music by Don McLean

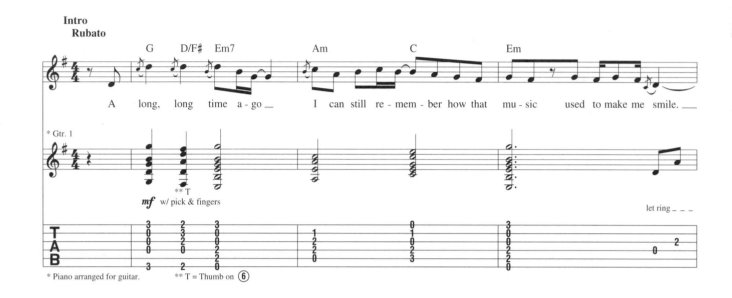

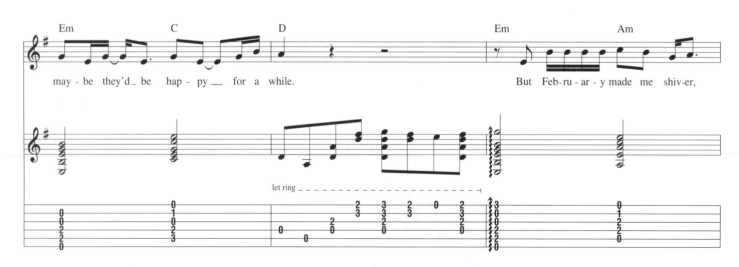

MCA Music Publishing

with ev-'ry pa-per I'd de-liv-er. Bad news on the door-step, I could-n't take one more step. I

can't re-mem-ber if I cried _____ when I read a-bout ___ his wid-owed bride.

Some-thing touched me deep in side, the day the mu - sic died.

Chorus
In Time
Moderately ♩ = 102

Gtr. 1 tacet

So, bye, _____ bye, Miss A - mer - i - can Pie. ___ Drove ___ my

Rhy. Fig. 1
Gtr. 2 (acous.)

mp w/ pick

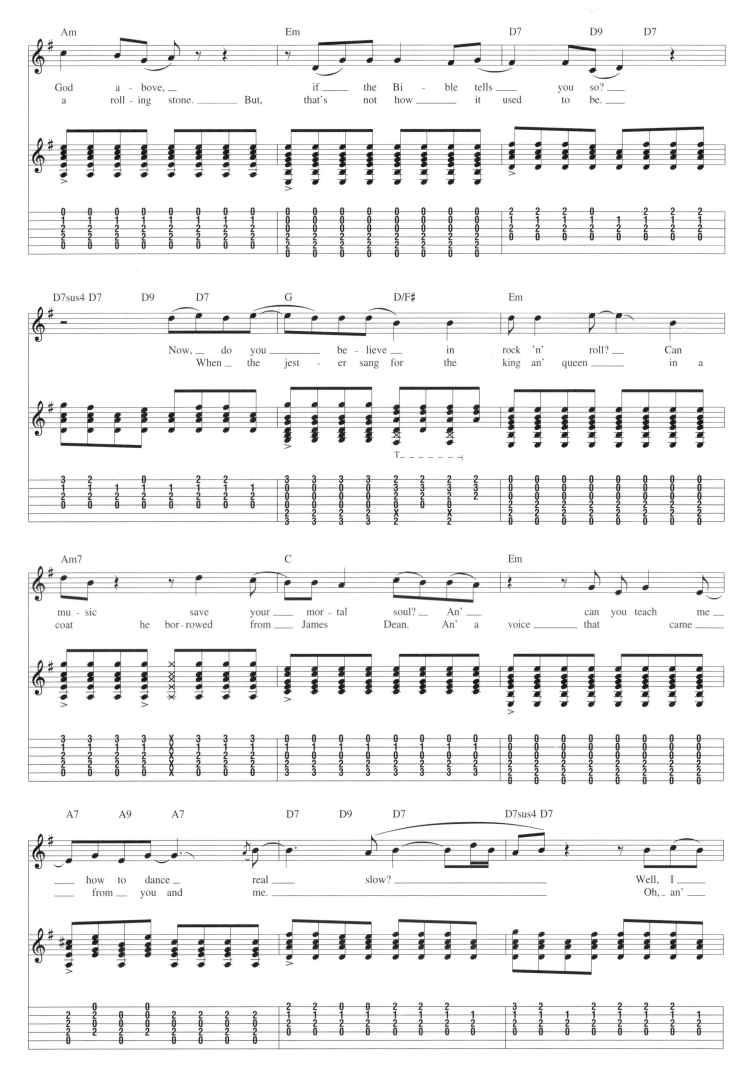

flew off with a fall-out shel-ter, eight _ miles _ high an' _ fall-in' fast. ___

It land-ed foul _ out _ on the grass. _ The play-ers tried _ for a

for-ward pass, _ with the jest - er on the side - lines in a cast. ___

Now, the half-time air _ was _ sweet per-fume, while the ser - geants _ played a

10

At Seventeen

Words and Music by Janis Ian

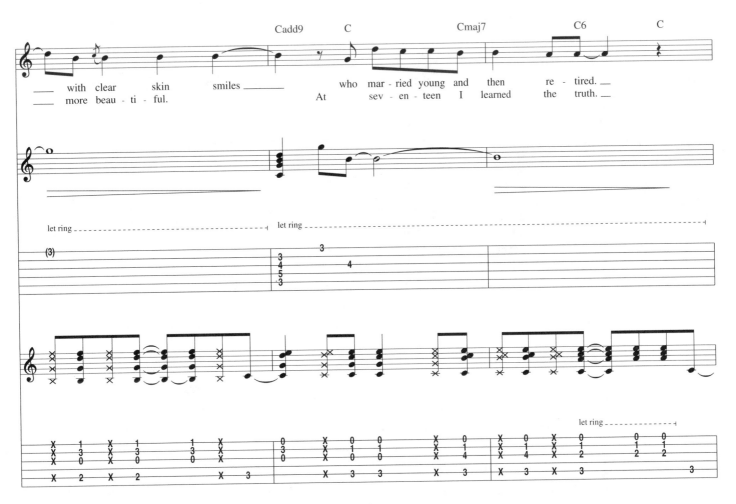

18

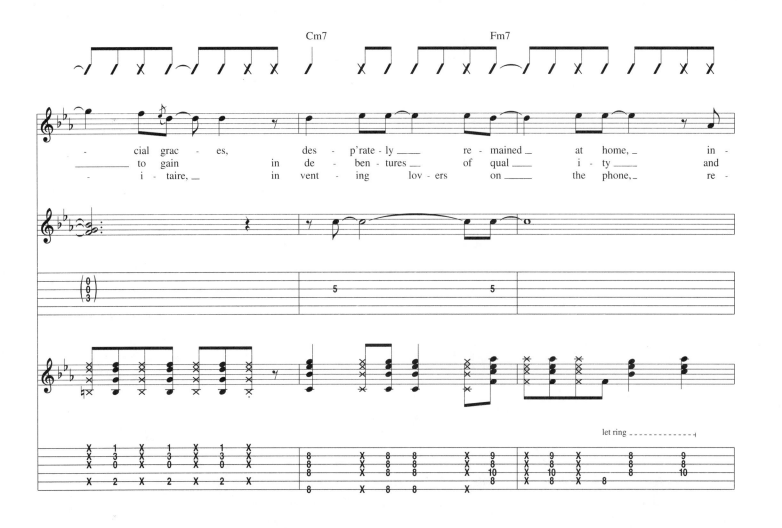

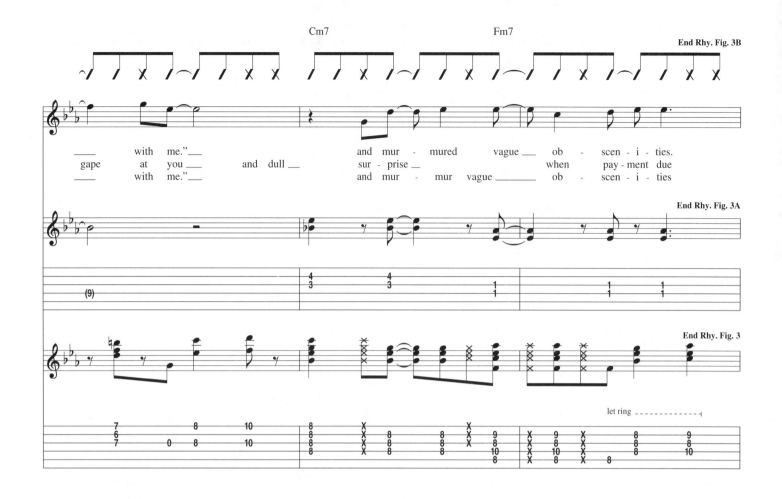

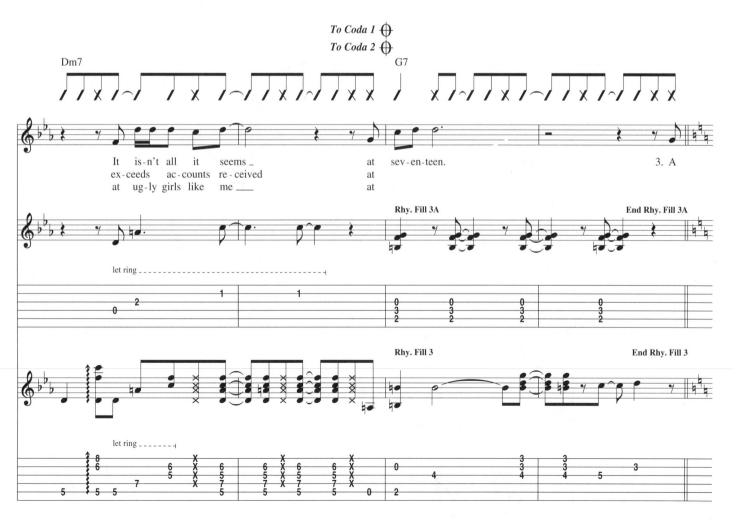

Verse

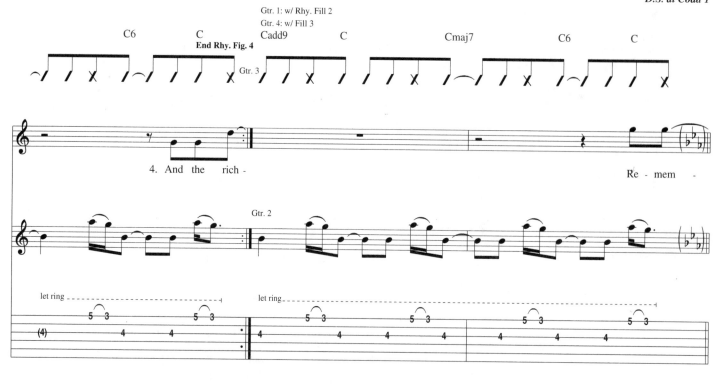

⊕ *Coda 1*

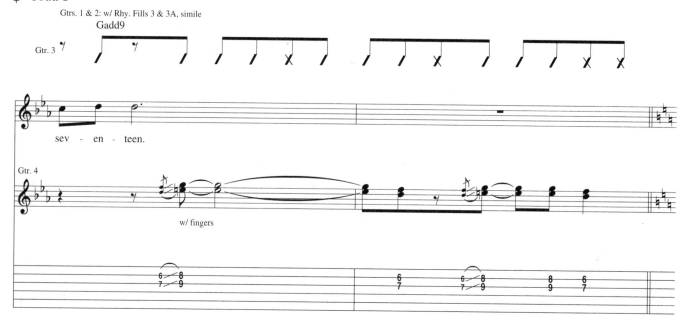

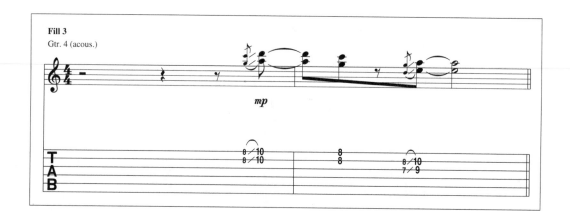

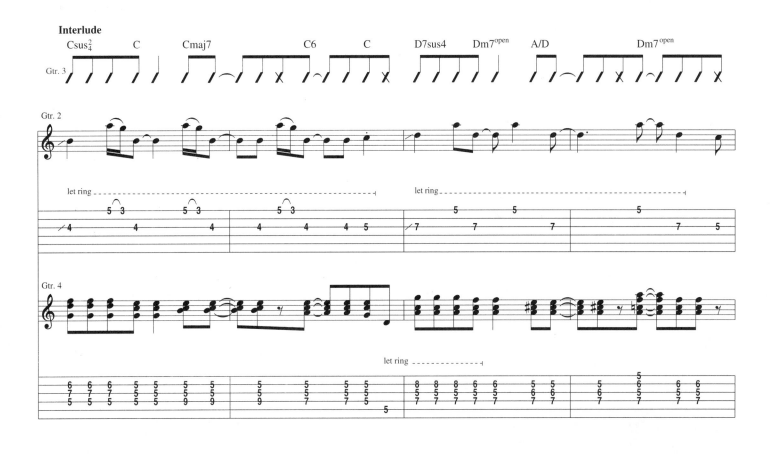

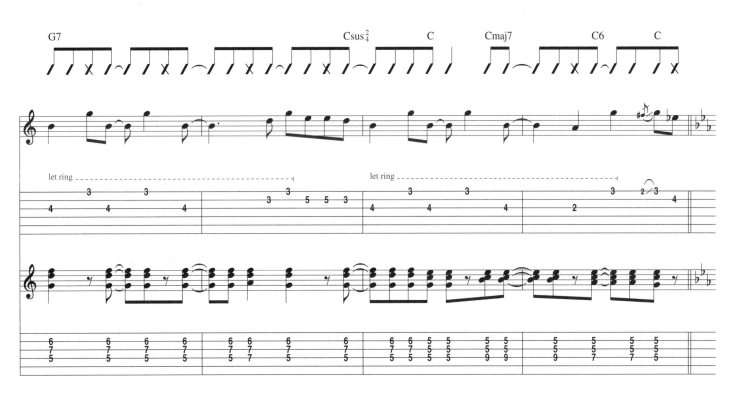

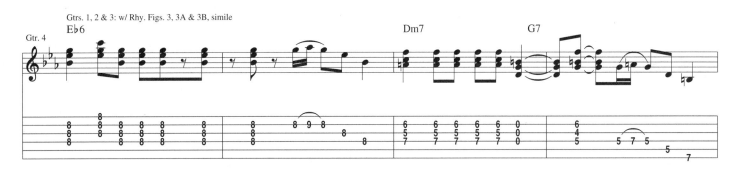

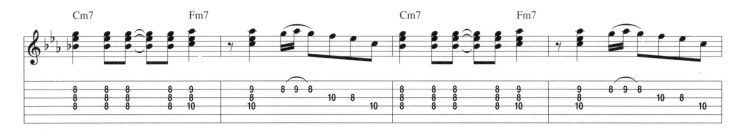

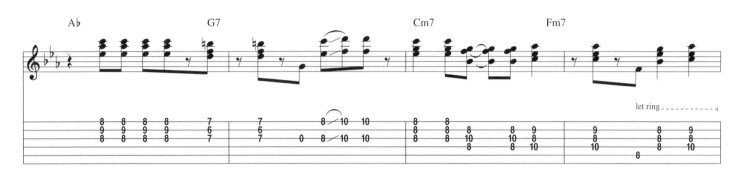

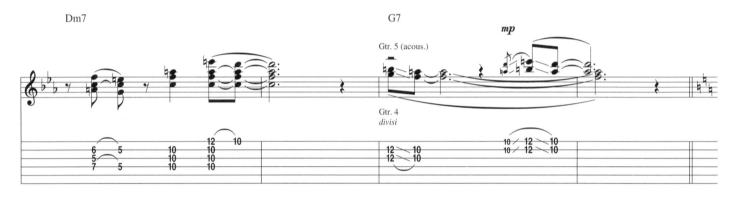

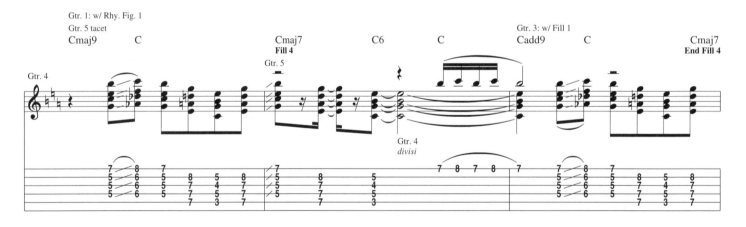

Verse

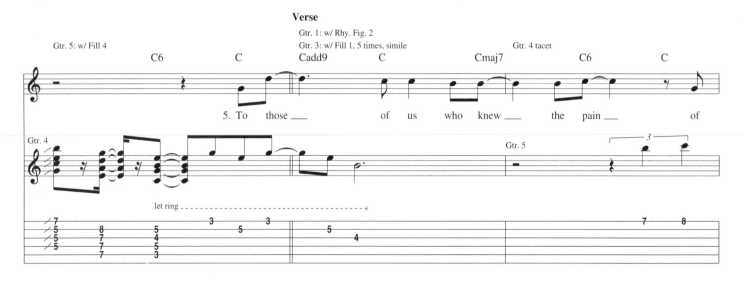

5. To those ___ of us who knew ___ the pain ___ of

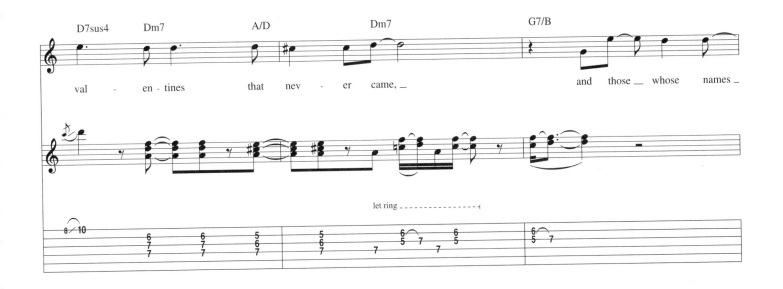

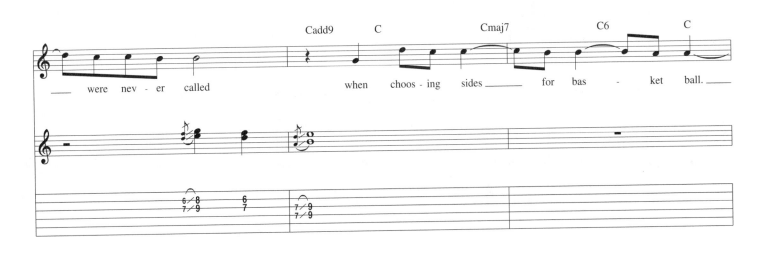

Verse

Gtr. 1: w/ Rhy. Fig. 2, 1st 8 meas.
Gtr. 3: w/ Rhy. Fig. 4, simile

the world ___ was _ young - er than _ to-day, _ and dreams _____ were all _ they gave _ for free

D.S. al Coda 2

Gtr. 1: w/ Rhy. Fill 2

to ug - ly duck - ling girls   like _____ me.   We all

⊕ *Coda 2*

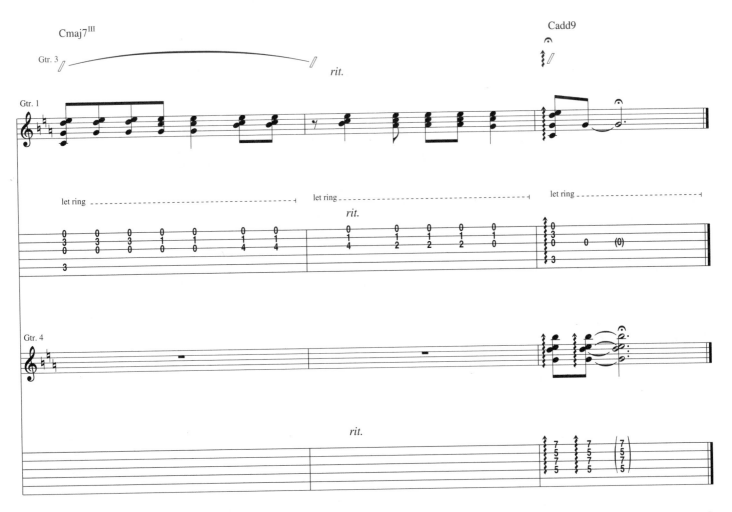

sev - en - teen.

The Best of My Love

Words and Music by John David Souther, Don Henley and Glenn Frey

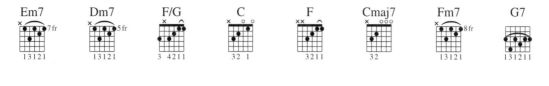

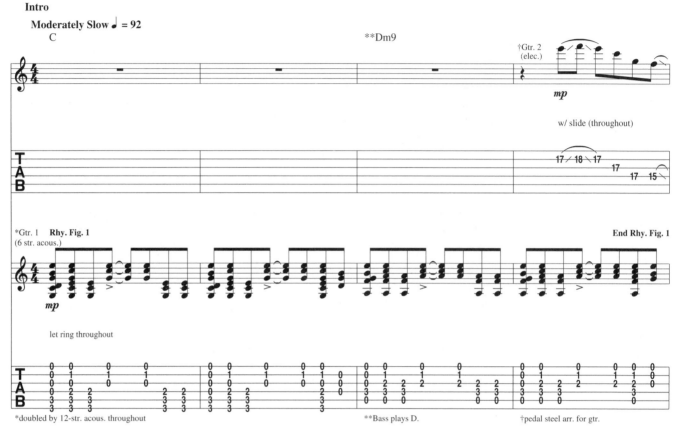

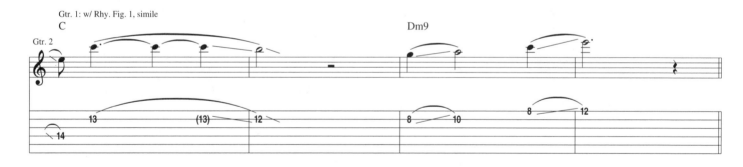

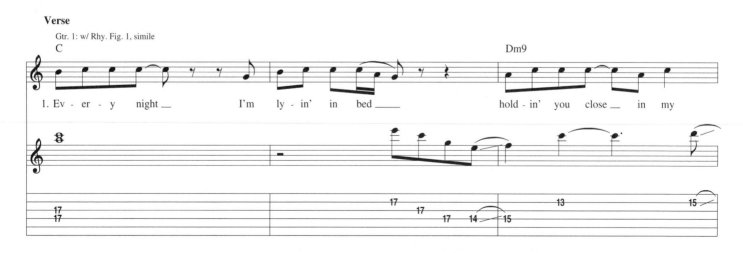

Gtr. 1: w/ Rhy. Fill 1

C

dreams. ___ Think - in' a - bout ___ all the things that we ___ said ___ and

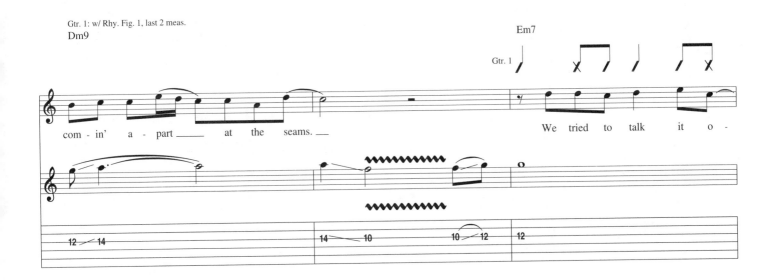

Gtr. 1: w/ Rhy. Fig. 1, last 2 meas.

Dm9   Em7

Gtr. 1

com - in' a - part ___ at the seams. ___   We tried to talk it o -

Dm7   Em7   F/G

(cont. in notation)

- ver ___ but the words come out ___ too ___ rough. ___   I

Rhy. Fill 1

Gtr. 1

let ring -

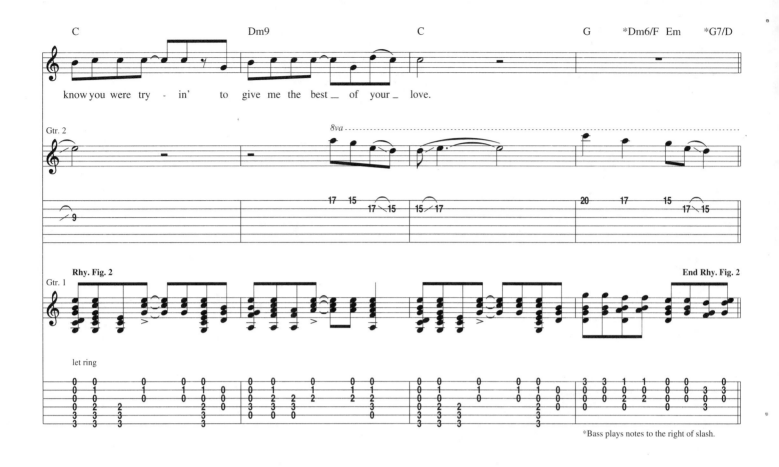

know you were try - in' to give me the best __ of your __ love.

*Bass plays notes to the right of slash.

Verse

2. Beau - ti - ful fac - es and loud emp - ty plac - es, look at the way that we live. __

Wast - in' our time __ on cheap talk and wine __ left us so lit - tle to give. __ That

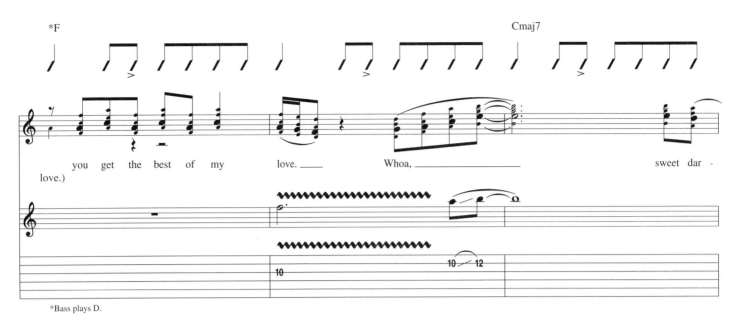

*F   Cmaj7

you get the best of my   love. _____   Whoa, _____   sweet dar -
love.)

*Bass plays D.

F   End Rhy. Fig. 4

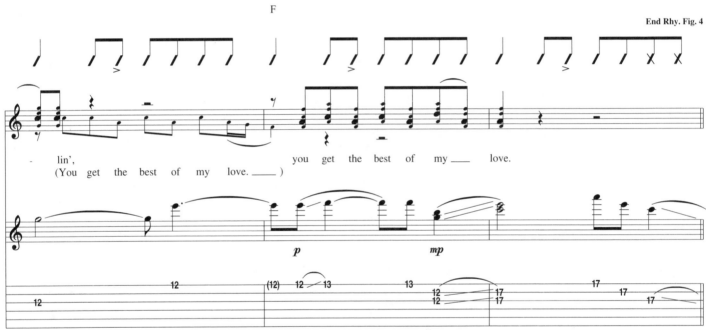

- lin',   you get the best of my ___ love.
(You get the best of my   love. ____)

Bridge

Fm7   Cmaj7

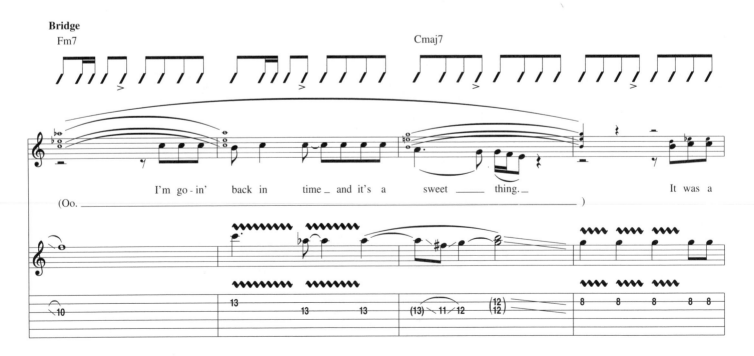

I'm go - in' back in time _ and it's a   sweet _____ thing. _   It was a
(Oo.   )

*Fret higher note w/o slide

Verse

34

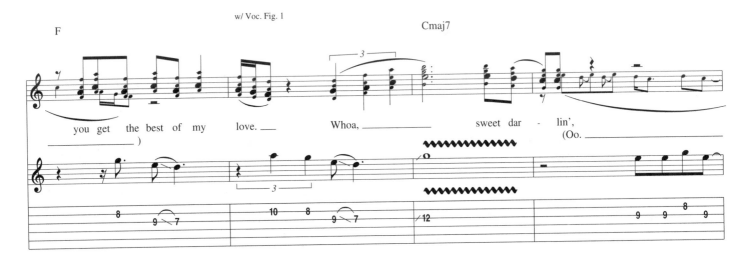

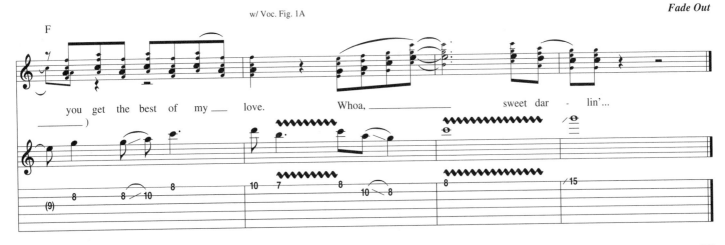

Fire and Rain

Words and Music by James Taylor

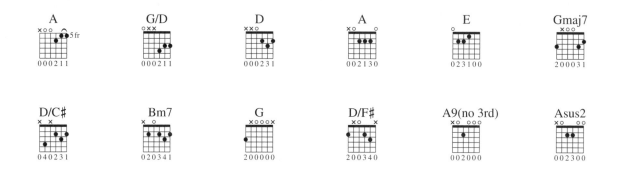

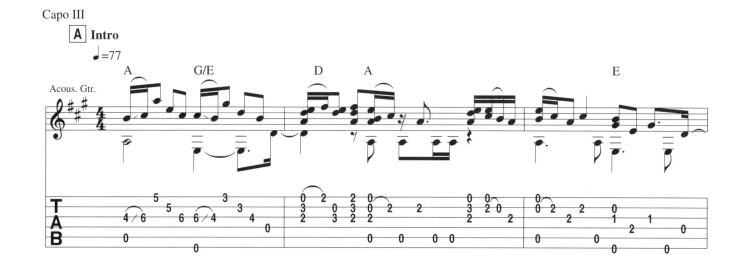

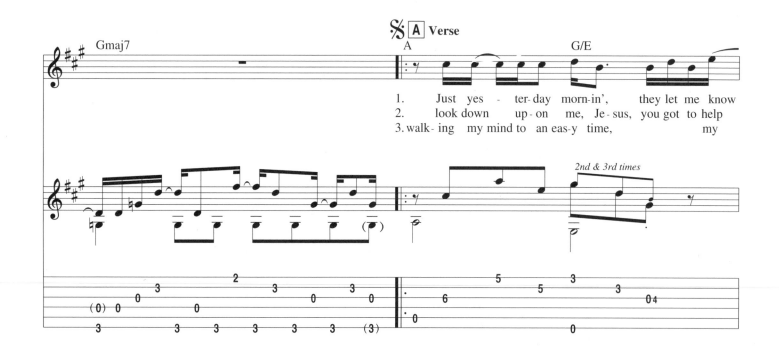

you were gone.
me make a stand.
back turned towards the sun.

Su - zanne, the plans they made _ put an
You've just got to see me through an -
Lord knows when the cold wind blows, it - 'll

end to you.
oth - er day.
turn your head a - round.

I walked out this morn - ing and I
My bo - dy's ach - ing and my
Well there's hours of time _ on the tel-e-phone line to

wrote down this song. _
time is at hand. _
talk a-bout things to come, _

I just can't re - mem - ber who to send _
I won't make it an - y
sweet dreams and fly-ing ma - chines in

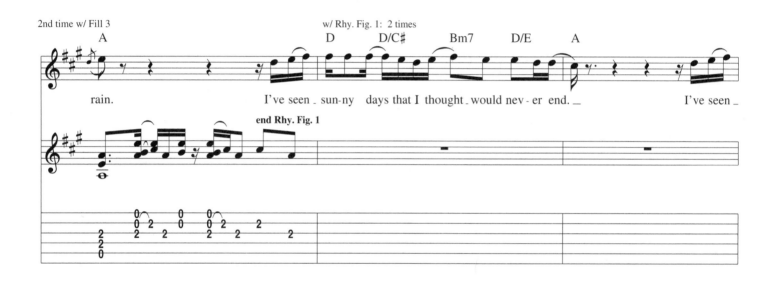

D **Outro**

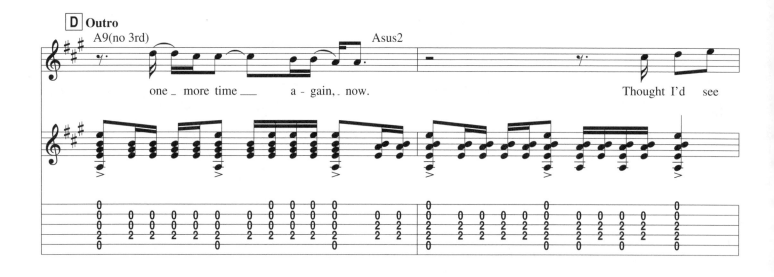

one _ more time ____ a - gain, _ now.   Thought I'd   see

Strumming simile

you   one _ more   time   a - gain.   There's _ just a few _

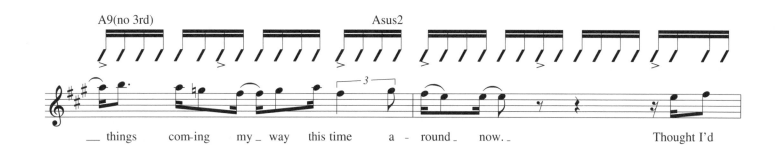

_ things   com-ing   my _ way   this time   a - round _ now. _   Thought I'd

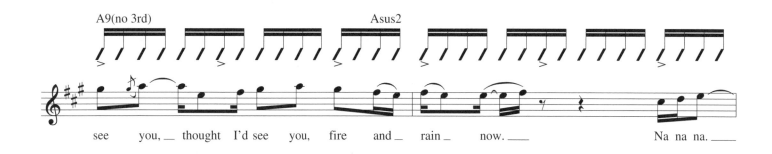

see   you, ___ thought I'd see   you,   fire   and _ rain _ now. ____   Na na na. ____

Fade

____   Na na   na ___ na   na na na na na ____ na.   Na na na ___ na na   na na   na.

Here Comes the Sun

Words and Music by George Harrison

*All notes tabbed on 7th fret are played as open strings

Leader of the Band

Words and Music by Dan Fogelberg

To Coda 1

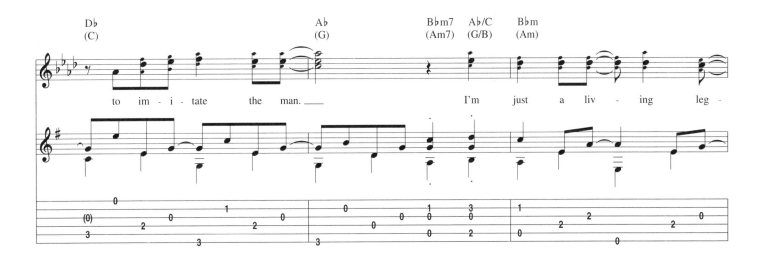

to im-i-tate the man.____ I'm just a liv-ing leg-

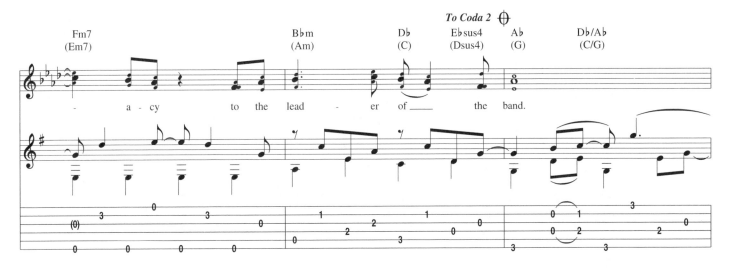

To Coda 2 ⊕

-a-cy to the lead-er of ____ the band.

D.S. al Coda 1

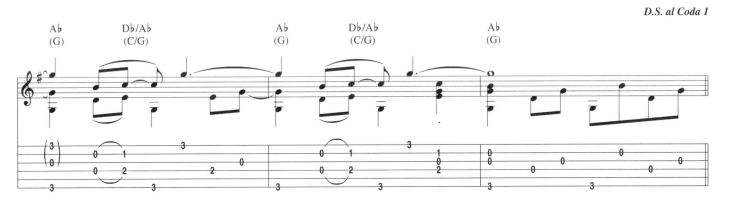

⊕ *Coda 1*

Interlude

Gtr. 1: w/ Rhy. Fig. 1

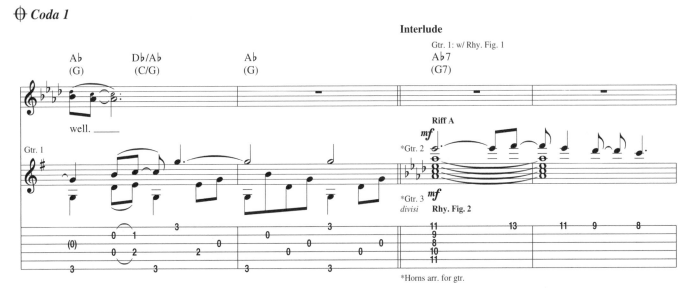

well.____

Gtr. 1

Riff A

mf

*Gtr. 2

*Gtr. 3 *mf*

divisi Rhy. Fig. 2

*Horns arr. for gtr.

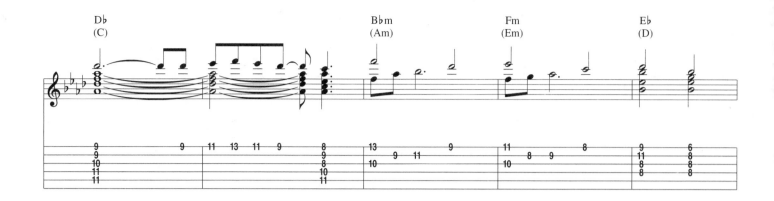

D.S. al Coda 2
(take 2nd ending)

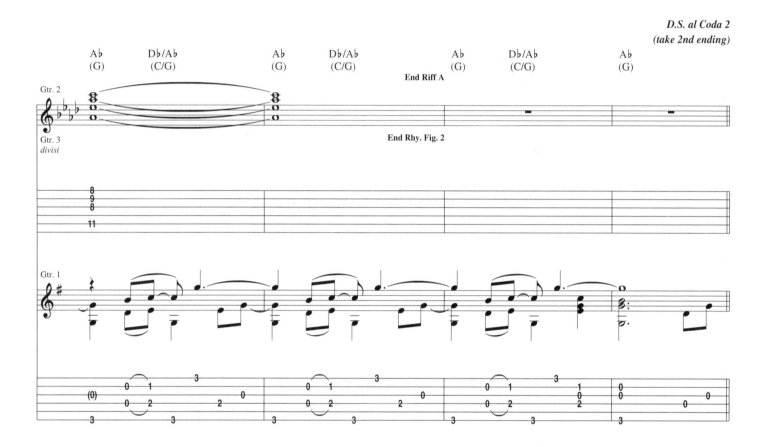

End Riff A

End Rhy. Fig. 2

⊕ Coda 2

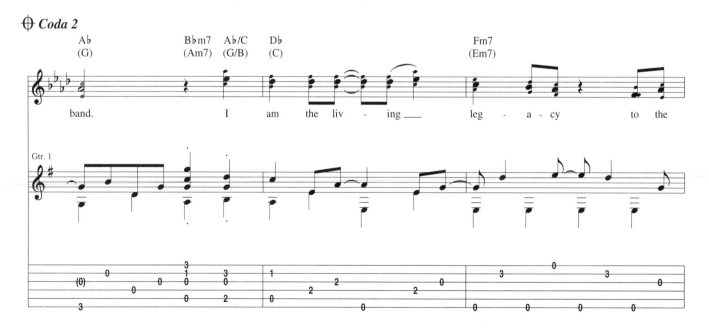

band.   I   am   the   liv - ing ___   leg - a - cy   to   the

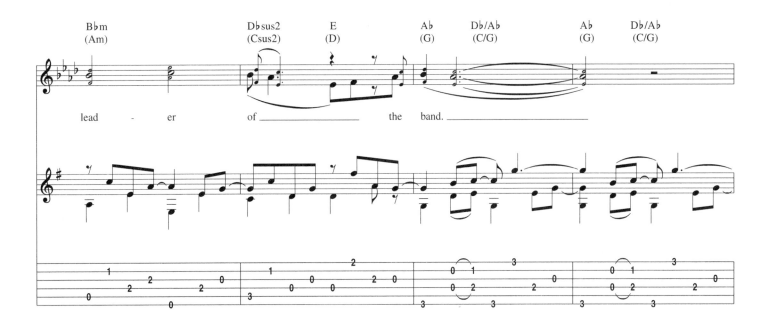

lead - er of _____ the band. _____

Outro

Gtrs. 2 & 3: w/ Riff A & Rhy. Fig. 2

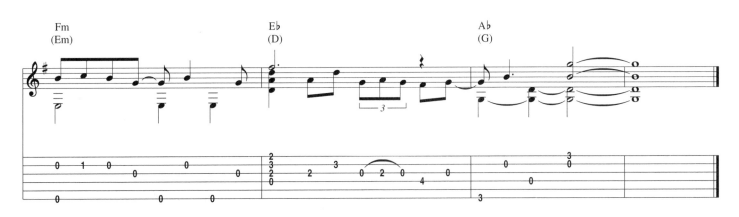

Leaving on a Jet Plane

Words and Music by John Denver

Southern Cross

Words and Music by Stephen Stills, Richard Curtis and Michael Curtis

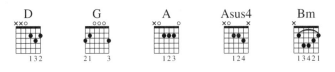

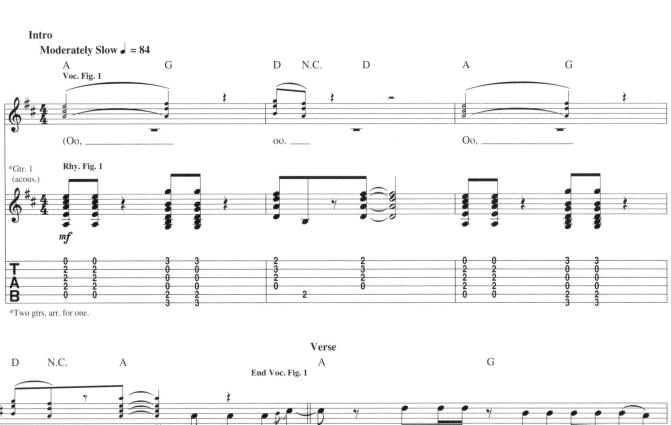

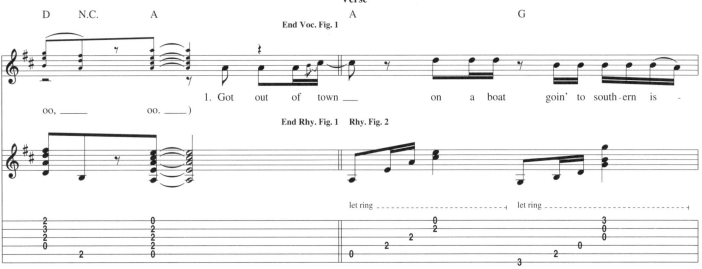

58

Chorus

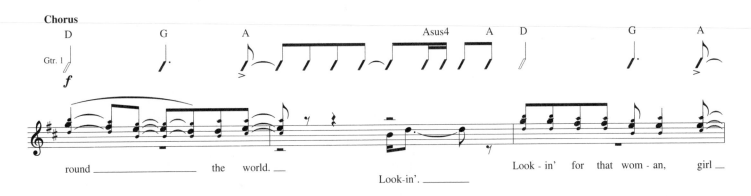

To Coda ⊕

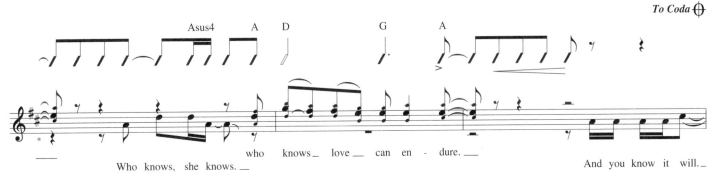

*downstem Voc. sung 1st time

Verse

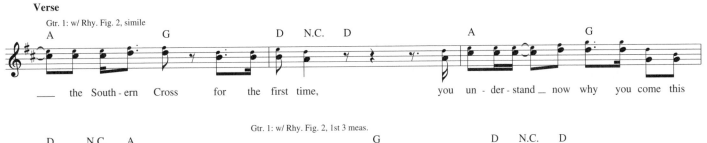

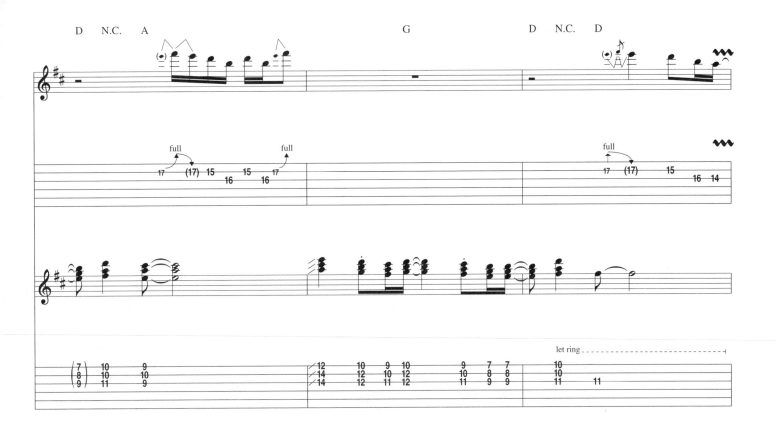

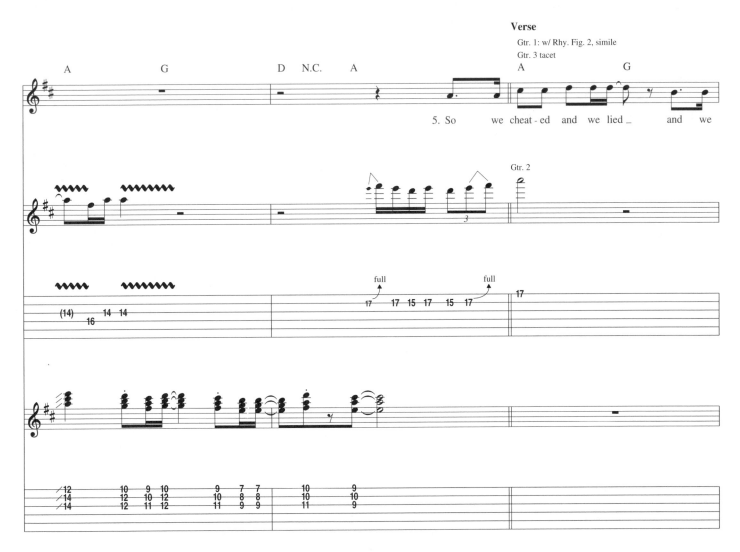

5. So we cheat-ed and we lied _ and we

Verse

Gtr. 1: w/ Rhy. Fig. 2, simile

Gtr. 3 tacet

test - ed. And we nev-er failed to fail; it was the eas-i-est thing to do. __

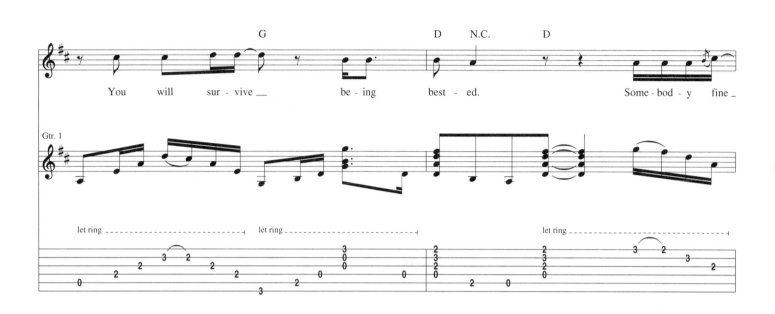

You will sur - vive __ be - ing best - ed. Some - bod - y fine __

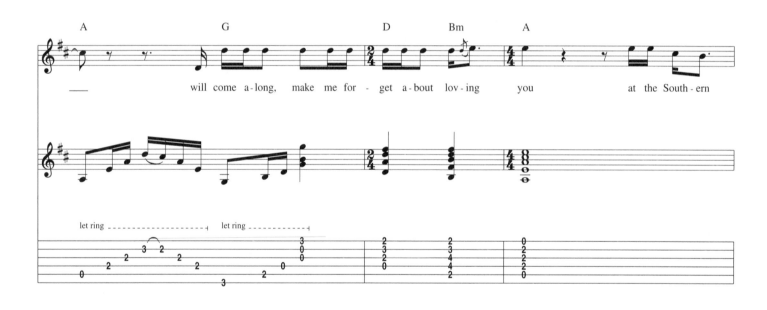

___ will come a - long, make me for - get a - bout lov - ing you at the South - ern

Summer Breeze

Words and Music by James Seals and Dash Crofts

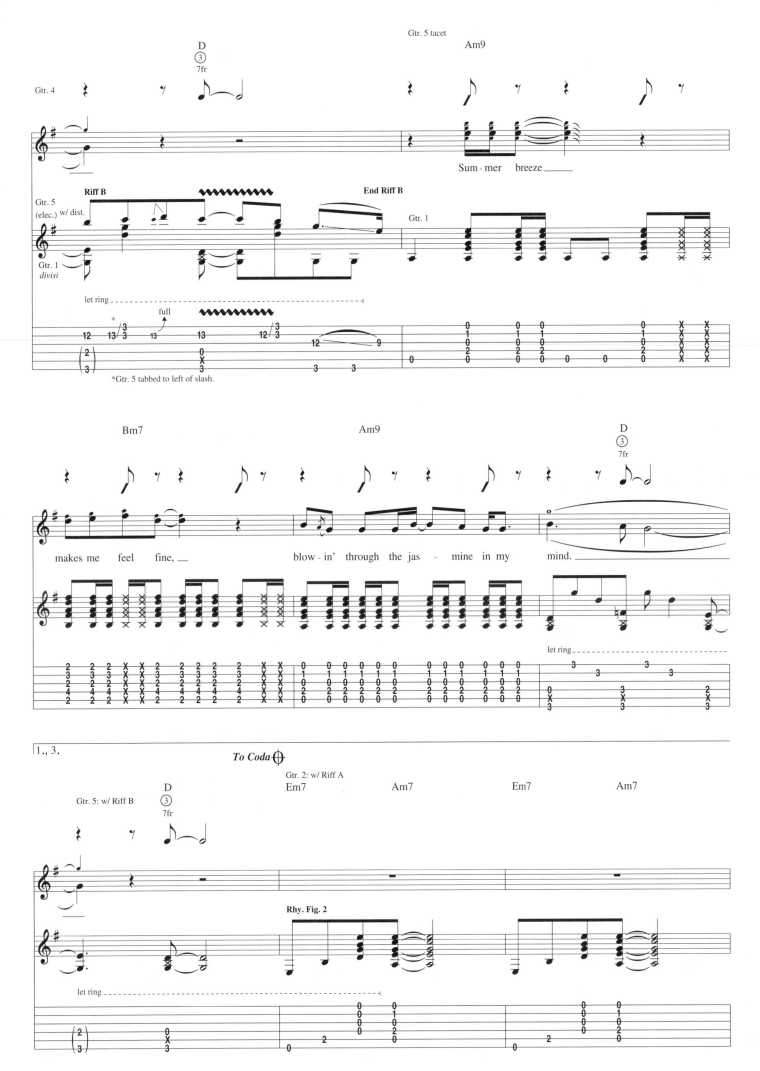

Bridge

Sweet days of sum-mer, the jas-mine's in bloom. Ju-ly is dressed up and

play-ing her tune. And I come home from a hard day's work and you're

D.S. al Coda
(take 1st ending)

wait-in' there, not a care in the world.

Coda

Repeat and Fade

Take Me Home, Country Roads

Words and Music by Bill Danoff, Taffy Nivert and John Denver

Blue Ridge Moun - tains, ___ Shen - an - do - ah Riv - er. ___
Min - er's la - dy, ___ Stran - ger to blue wa - ter. ___

simile on repeat

let ring

___ Life is old ___ there, ___ old - er than ___ the ___
___ Dark and dust - y, ___ paint - ed on ___ the ___

let ring

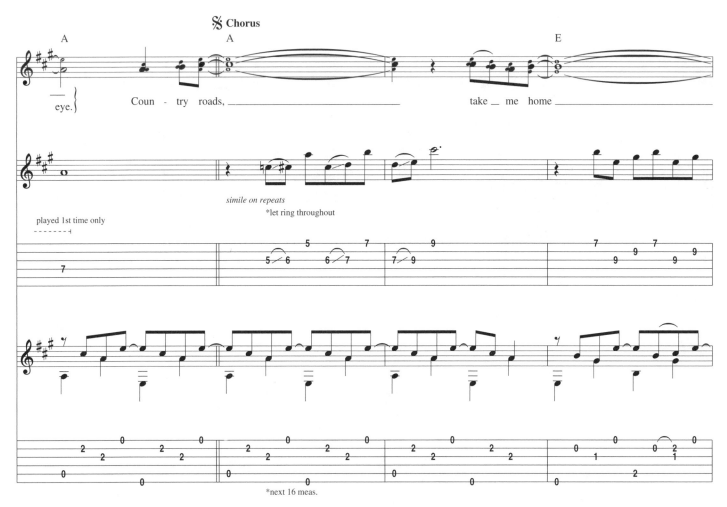

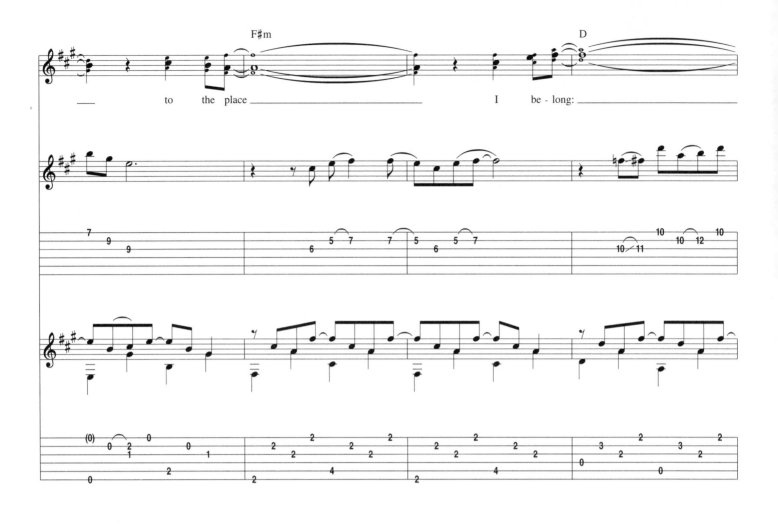

to the place   I   be - long:

West Vir - gin - ia,   moun - tain mom - ma.

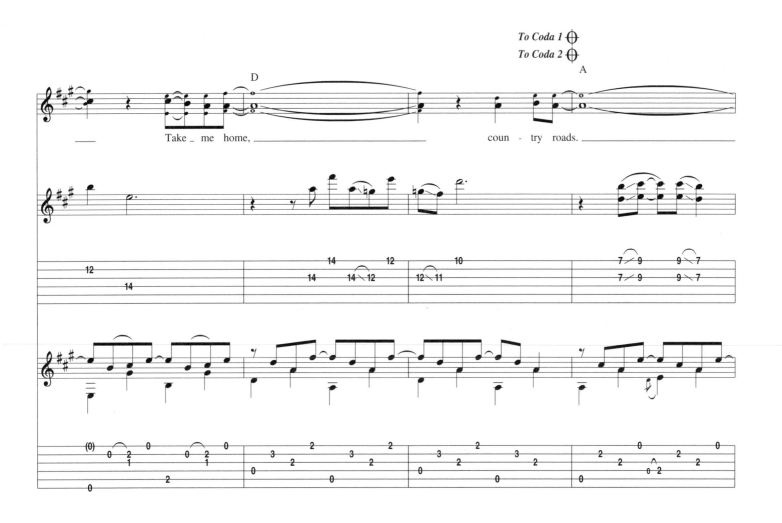

Take me home, coun - try roads.

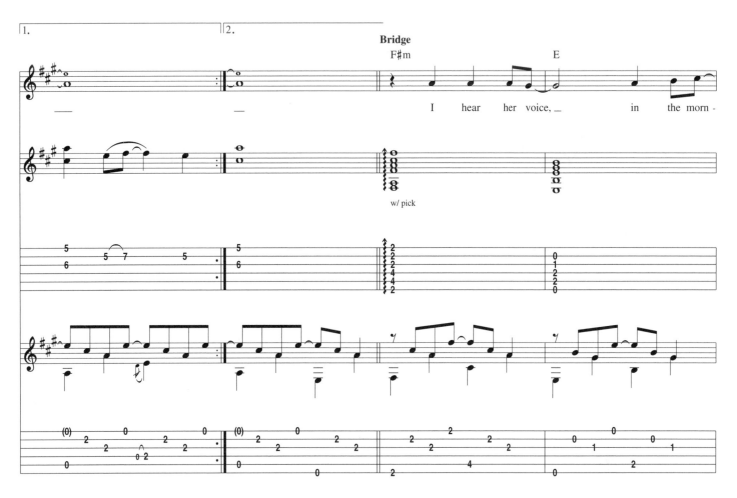

Bridge

F#m   E

I hear her voice, in the morn -

w/ pick

-in' hour _ she calls _____ me. The ra - di - o _____ re - minds _____ me of my

home far a - way. _____ And driv - in' down _ the road _____ I get a feel-

in' that I should have been ___ home yes - ter - day, ___

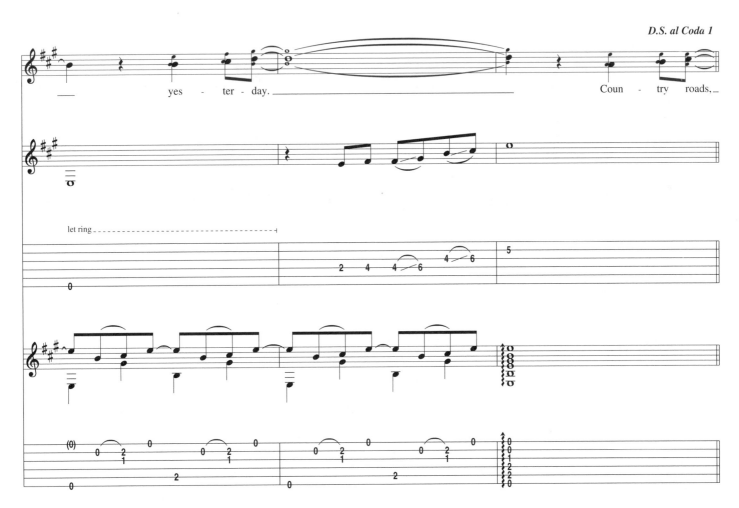

D.S. al Coda 1

yes - ter - day. ___ Coun - try roads, ___

⊕ *Coda 1*

Coun - try roads, _____

*vocals doubled till end

⊕ *Coda 2*

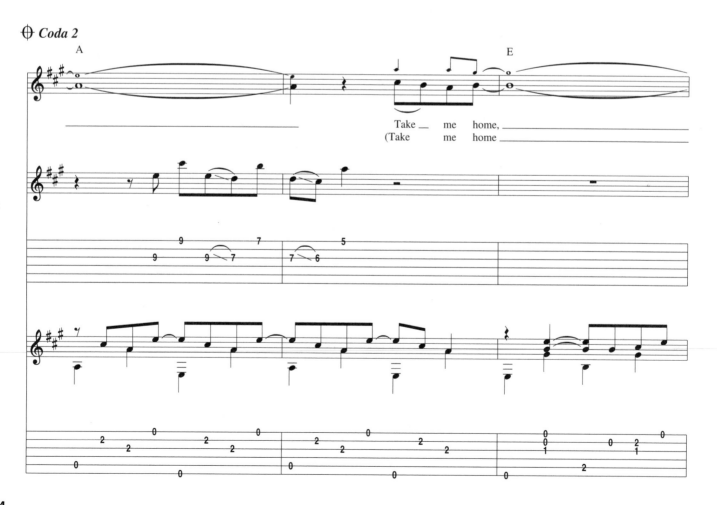

Take _ me home, _____
(Take me home _____

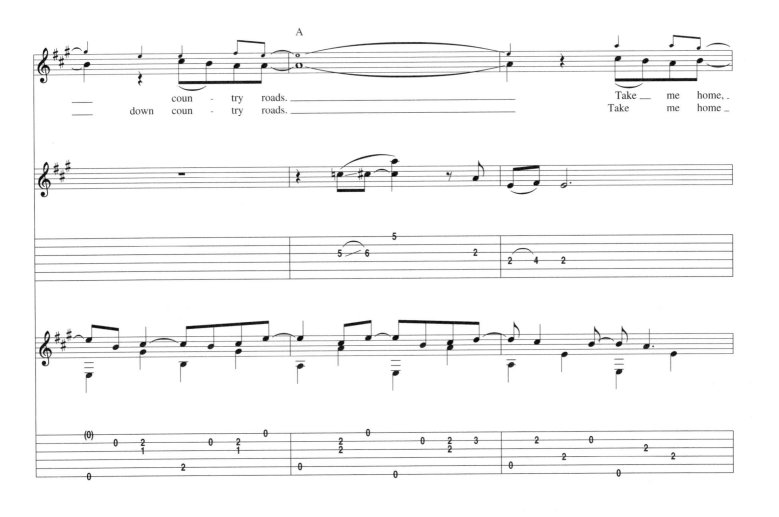

coun - try roads. _____ Take __ me home, __
down coun - try roads. _____ Take me home __

coun - try roads. _____
down coun - try roads. _____)

Taxi

Words and Music by Harry Chapin

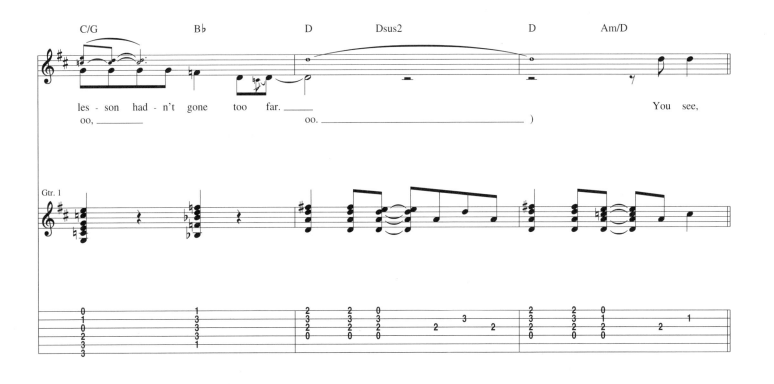

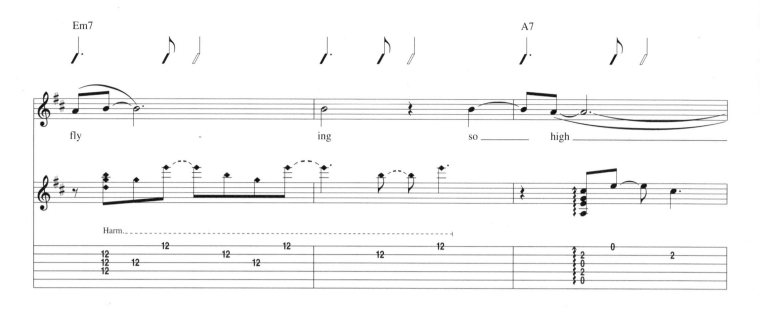

fly - ing so high

Outro

Gtr. 1: w/ Rhy. Fig. 2, till fade

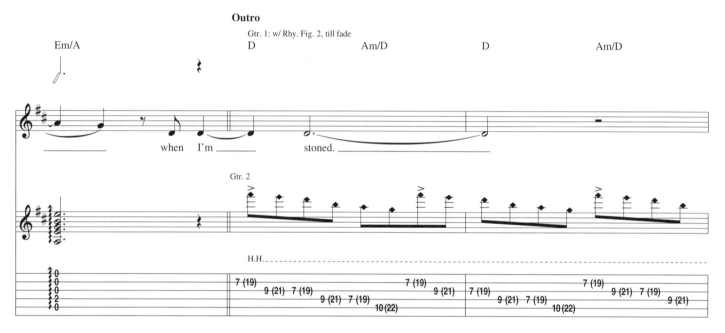

when I'm stoned.

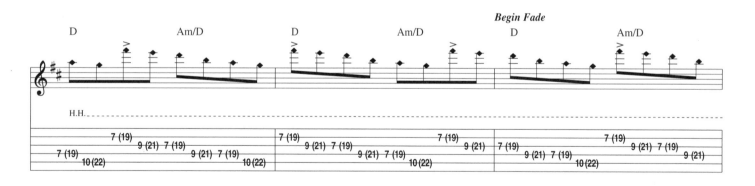

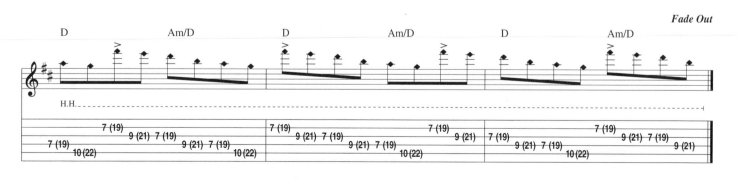

Turn! Turn! Turn!

(To Everything There Is a Season)

Words from the Book of Ecclesiastes
Adaption and Music by Pete Seeger

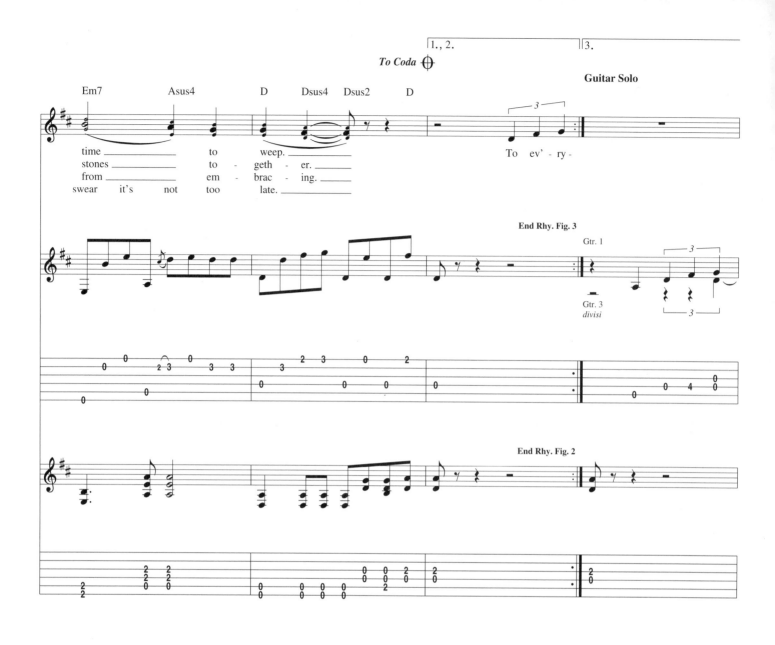

time _____ to weep. _____
stones _____ to - geth - er. _____
from _____ em - brac - ing. _____
swear it's not too late. _____

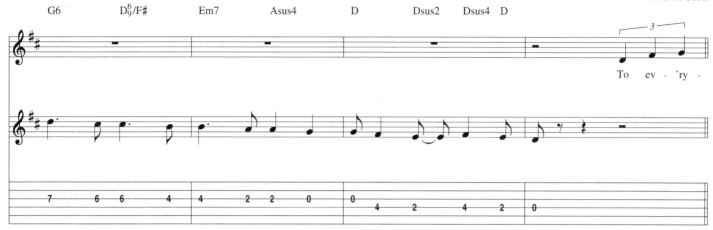

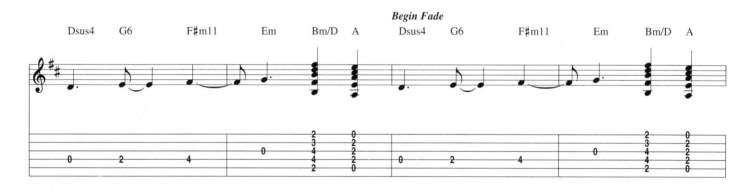

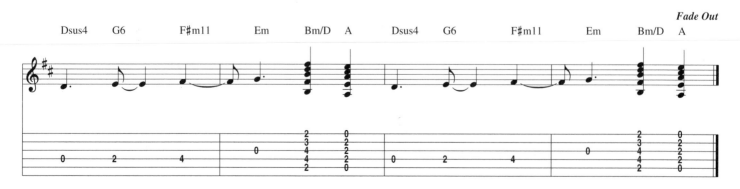

You're Only Lonely

Words and Music by John David Souther

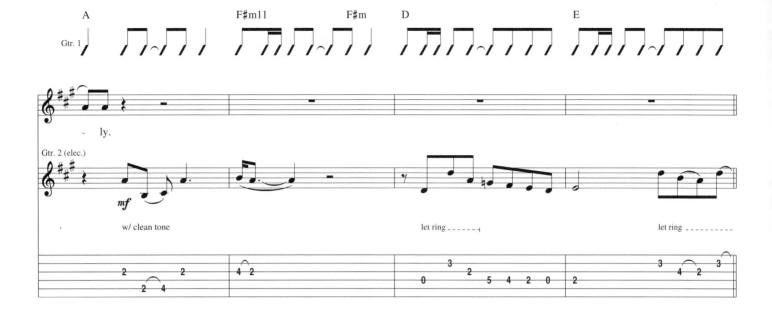

Verse

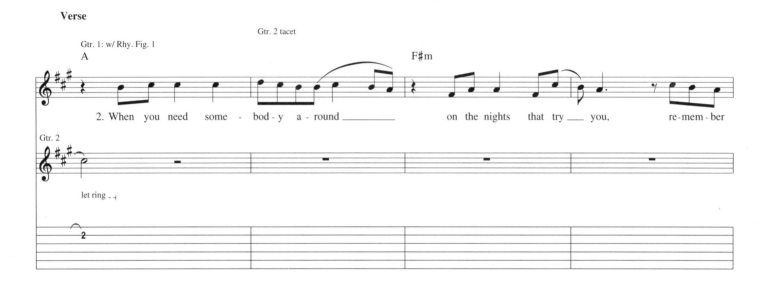

2. When you need some-bod-y a-round on the nights that try __ you, re-mem-ber

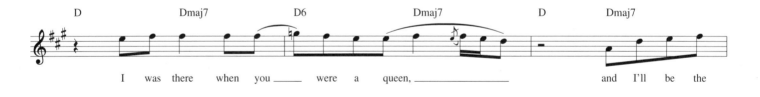

I was there when you __ were a queen, __ and I'll be the

last one there be-side __ you. __ So you can call out my name __

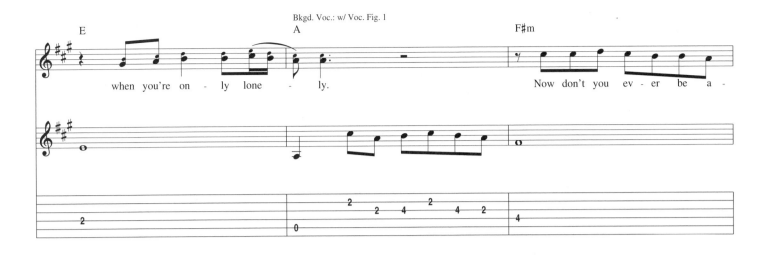
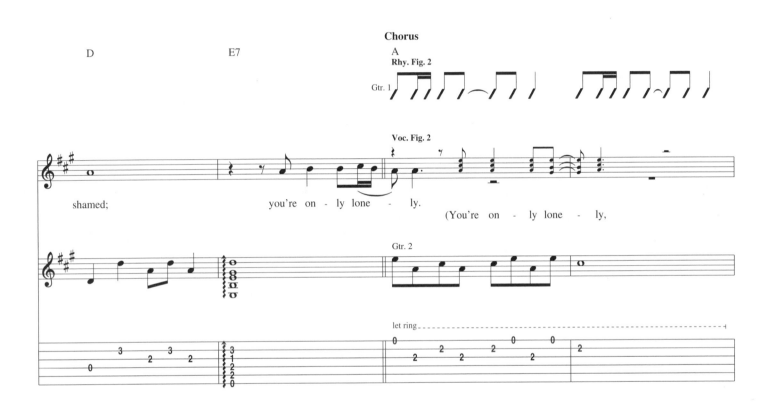

Verse

Gtr. 1: w/ Rhy. Fig. 1

E

A

End Rhy. Fig. 2

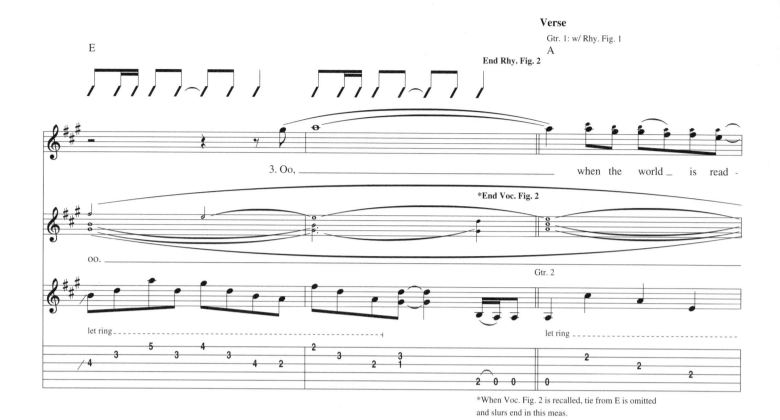

3. Oo, _____ when the world _ is read -

oo. _____

*End Voc. Fig. 2

Gtr. 2

let ring

let ring

*When Voc. Fig. 2 is recalled, tie from E is omitted
and slurs end in this meas.

F#m   D   Dmaj7

\- y to fall _____ on your lit - tle shoul - ders, and when you're feel - in' lone -

Oo, _____

let ring   let ring   let ring

D6   Dmaj7   D   Dmaj7   D6   Dmaj7   A

\- ly and _ small, _____ you need some - bod - y there to hold _ you.

oo,   oo.

let ring

98

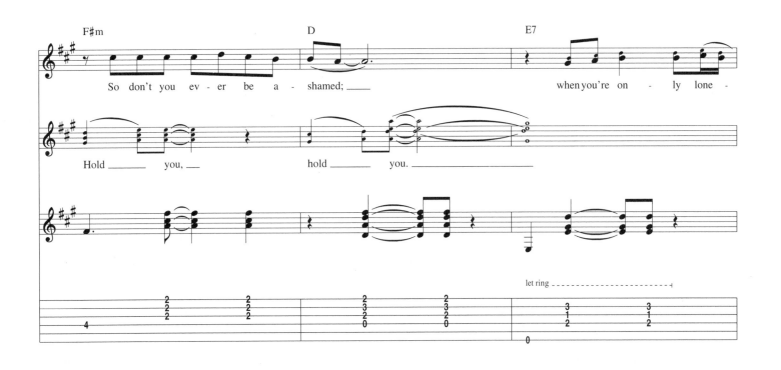

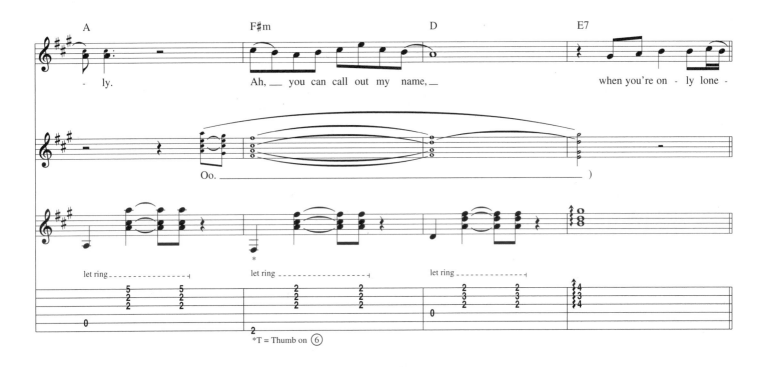

Outro-Chorus

Gtr. 1: w/ Rhy. Fig. 2, till fade

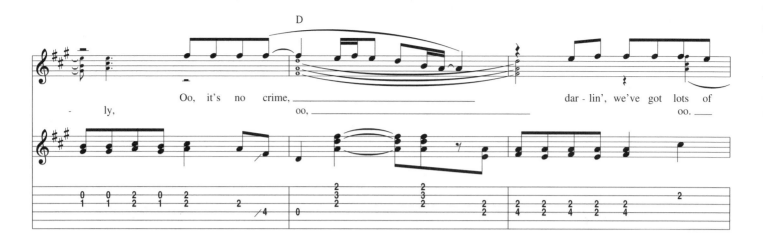

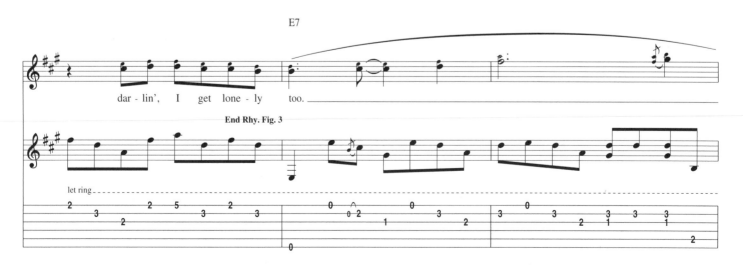

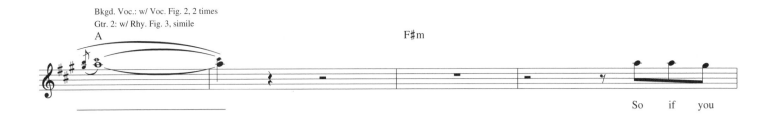

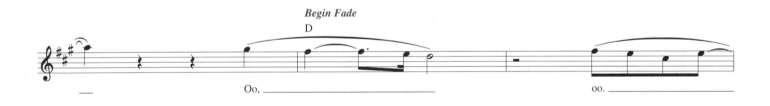

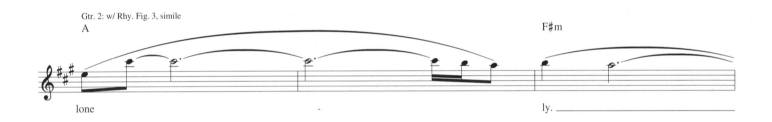

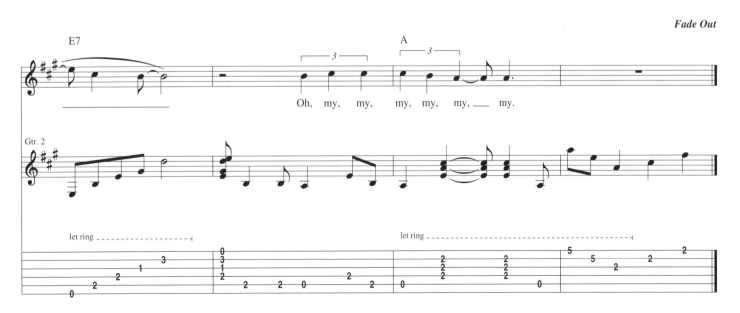

You're So Vain

Words and Music by Carly Simon

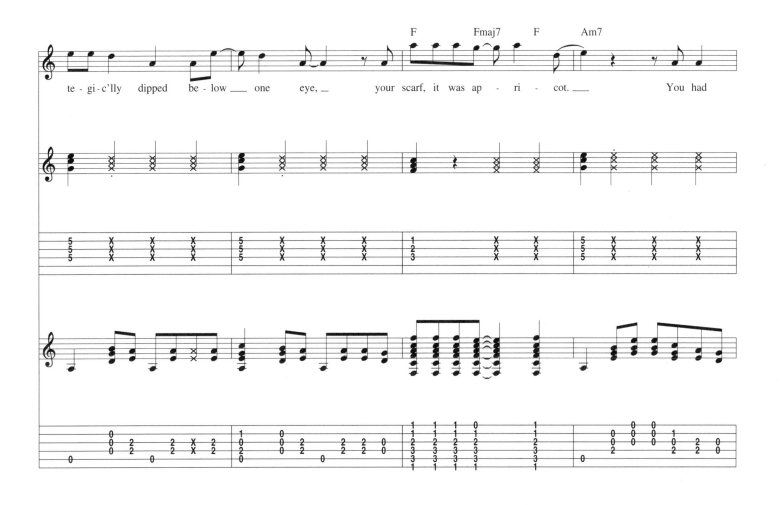

te - gi - c'lly dipped be - low ___ one eye, ___ your scarf, it was ap - ri - cot. ___ You had

one eye ___ in ___ the mir - ror as ___ you watched your - self ___ ga - votte. ___ And ___ all the girls ___

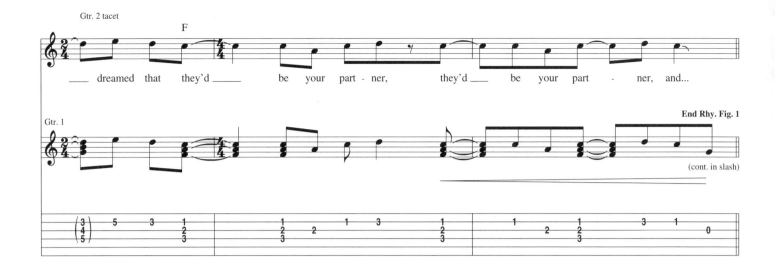

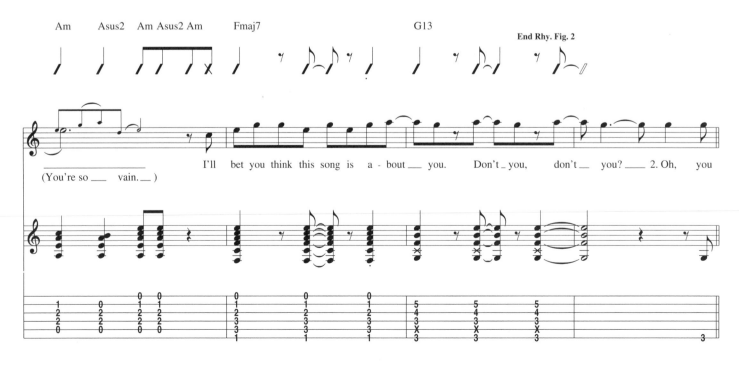

things you loved,___ and one of them ___ was ___ me. ___ I ___ had some dreams, ___ they were clouds___
all the time, ___ and when you're not, ___ you're with ___ some un - der-world spy ___ or the wife

let ring

Chorus

Gtr. 1: w/ Rhy. Fig. 2, simile

___ in my cof - fee, clouds ___ in my cof - fee, and.. You're___ so ___ vain.
___ of a close friend, wife ___ of a close ___ friend, and...

Rhy. Fig. 2A

Gtr. 2

You prob - b'ly think this song is a - bout ___ you. You're___ so ___ vain,___

let ring

Rhy. Fill 2

Gtr. 2

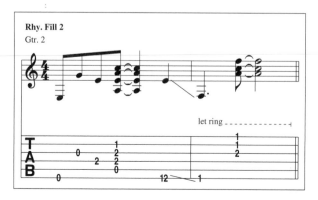

let ring

*Wear slide on pinky. Use where indicated.

Gtrs. 1 & 2: w/ Rhy. Figs. 2 & 2A, simile
Gtr. 3 tacet

You're _ so _ vain, _ you prob-b'ly think this song is a-bout _ you. You're _ so _ vain,

I'll bet you think this song is a-bout _ you. Don't _ you, don't _ you? 3. Well, I
(You're so _ vain. _)

Coda

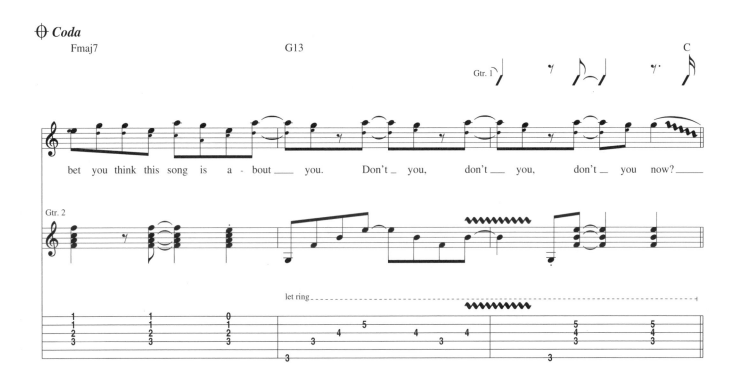

bet you think this song is a-bout _ you. Don't _ you, don't _ you, don't _ you now? _

let ring _ _ _ _ _ _ _ _ _

Outro

Gtr. 1: w/ Rhy. Fig. 2, 1st 4 meas., simile, till fade

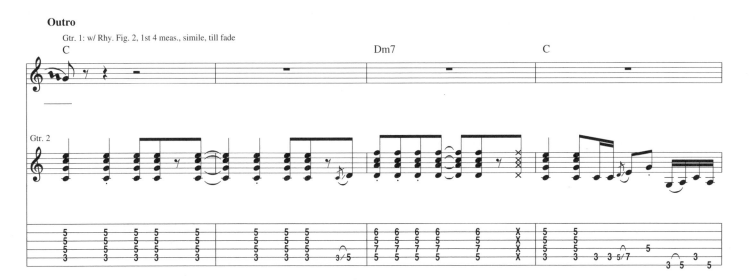

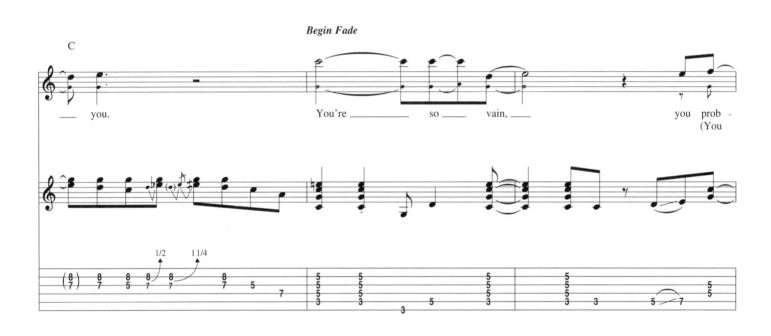

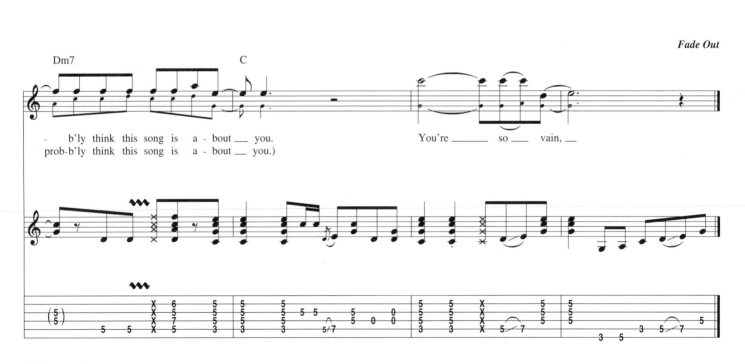

Guitar Notation Legend

Guitar Music can be notated three different ways: on a *musical staff*, in *tablature*, and in *rhythm slashes*.

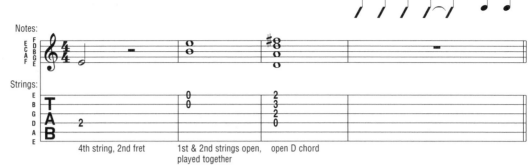

RHYTHM SLASHES are written above the staff. Strum chords in the rhythm indicated. Use the chord diagrams found at the top of the first page of the transcription for the appropriate chord voicings. Round noteheads indicate single notes.

THE MUSICAL STAFF shows pitches and rhythms and is divided by bar lines into measures. Pitches are named after the first seven letters of the alphabet.

TABLATURE graphically represents the guitar fingerboard. Each horizontal line represents a string, and each number represents a fret.

4th string, 2nd fret | 1st & 2nd strings open, played together | open D chord

---

HALF-STEP BEND: Strike the note and bend up 1/2 step.

WHOLE-STEP BEND: Strike the note and bend up one step.

GRACE NOTE BEND: Strike the note and bend up as indicated. The first note does not take up any time.

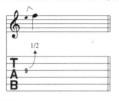

SLIGHT (MICROTONE) BEND: Strike the note and bend up 1/4 step.

BEND AND RELEASE: Strike the note and bend up as indicated, then release back to the original note. Only the first note is struck.

PRE-BEND: Bend the note as indicated, then strike it.

VIBRATO: The string is vibrated by rapidly bending and releasing the note with the fretting hand.

WIDE VIBRATO: The pitch is varied to a greater degree by vibrating with the fretting hand.

HAMMER-ON: Strike the first (lower) note with one finger, then sound the higher note (on the same string) with another finger by fretting it without picking.

PULL-OFF: Place both fingers on the notes to be sounded. Strike the first note and without picking, pull the finger off to sound the second (lower) note.

LEGATO SLIDE: Strike the first note and then slide the same fret-hand finger up or down to the second note. The second note is not struck.

SHIFT SLIDE: Same as legato slide, except the second note is struck.

TRILL: Very rapidly alternate between the notes indicated by continuously hammering on and pulling off.

TAPPING: Hammer ("tap") the fret indicated with the pick-hand index or middle finger and pull off to the note fretted by the fret hand.

NATURAL HARMONIC: Strike the note while the fret-hand lightly touches the string directly over the fret indicated.

PINCH HARMONIC: The note is fretted normally and a harmonic is produced by adding the edge of the thumb or the tip of the index finger of the pick hand to the normal pick attack.

PICK SCRAPE: The edge of the pick is rubbed down (or up) the string, producing a scratchy sound.

MUFFLED STRINGS: A percussive sound is produced by laying the fret hand across the string(s) without depressing, and striking them with the pick hand.

PALM MUTING: The note is partially muted by the pick hand lightly touching the string(s) just before the bridge.

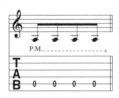

RAKE: Drag the pick across the strings indicated with a single motion.

TREMOLO PICKING: The note is picked as rapidly and continuously as possible.

VIBRATO BAR DIVE AND RETURN: The pitch of the note or chord is dropped a specified number of steps (in rhythm) then returned to the original pitch.

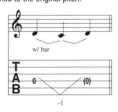

VIBRATO BAR SCOOP: Depress the bar just before striking the note, then quickly release the bar.

VIBRATO BAR DIP: Strike the note and then immediately drop a specified number of steps, then release back to the original pitch.

RECORDED VERSIONS
The Best Note-For-Note Transcriptions Available

RECORDED VERSIONS GUITAR

ALL BOOKS INCLUDE TABLATURE

00694909 Aerosmith – Get A Grip	$19.95
00690199 Aerosmith – Nine Lives	$19.95
00690146 Aerosmith – Toys in the Attic	$19.95
00694865 Alice In Chains – Dirt	$19.95
00660225 Alice In Chains – Facelift	$19.95
00694925 Alice In Chains – Jar Of Flies/Sap	$19.95
00694932 Allman Brothers Band – Volume 1	$24.95
00694933 Allman Brothers Band – Volume 2	$24.95
00694934 Allman Brothers Band – Volume 3	$24.95
00694877 Chet Atkins – Guitars For All Seasons	$19.95
00694918 Randy Bachman Collection	$22.95
00694880 Beatles – Abbey Road	$19.95
00694891 Beatles – Revolver	$19.95
00694863 Beatles – Sgt. Pepper's Lonely Hearts Club Band	$19.95
00690174 Beck – Mellow Gold	$17.95
00690175 Beck – Odelay	$17.95
00694931 Belly – Star	$19.95
00694884 The Best of George Benson	$19.95
00692385 Chuck Berry	$19.95
00692200 Black Sabbath – We Sold Our Soul For Rock 'N' Roll	$19.95
00690115 Blind Melon – Soup	$19.95
00690241 Bloodhound Gang – One Fierce Beer Coaster	$19.95
00690028 Blue Oyster Cult – Cult Classics	$19.95
00690219 Blur	$19.95
00690173 Tracy Bonham – The Burdens Of Being Upright	$17.95
00694935 Boston: Double Shot Of	$22.95
00690237 Meredith Brooks – Blurring the Edges	$19.95
00690043 Cheap Trick – Best Of	$19.95
00690171 Chicago – Definitive Guitar Collection	$22.95
00690010 Eric Clapton – From The Cradle	$19.95
00660139 Eric Clapton – Journeyman	$19.95
00694869 Eric Clapton – Live Acoustic	$19.95
00694873 Eric Clapton – Timepieces	$19.95
00694896 John Mayall/Eric Clapton – Bluesbreakers	$19.95
00694940 Counting Crows – August & Everything After	$19.95
00690197 Counting Crows – Recovering the Satellites	$19.95
00690118 Cranberries – The Best of	$19.95
00694941 Crash Test Dummies – God Shuffled His Feet	$19.95
00694840 Cream – Disraeli Gears	$19.95
00690007 Danzig 4	$19.95
00690184 DC Talk – Jesus Freak	$19.95
00660186 Alex De Grassi Guitar Collection	$19.95
00694831 Derek And The Dominos – Layla & Other Assorted Love Songs	$19.95
00690187 Dire Straits – Brothers In Arms	$19.95
00690191 Dire Straits – Money For Nothing	$24.95
00690182 Dishwalla – Pet Your Friends	$19.95
00660089 Willie Dixon – Master Blues Composer	$24.95
00690089 Foo Fighters	$19.95
00690042 Robben Ford Blues Collection	$19.95
00694920 Free – Best Of	$18.95
00690222 G3 Live – Satriani, Vai, Johnson	$22.95
00694894 Frank Gambale – The Great Explorers	$19.95
00694807 Danny Gatton – 88 Elmira St	$19.95
00690127 Goo Goo Dolls – A Boy Named Goo	$19.95
00690117 John Gorka Collection	$19.95
00690114 Buddy Guy Collection Vol. A-J	$19.95
00690193 Buddy Guy Collection Vol. L-Y	$19.95
00694798 George Harrison Anthology	$19.95
00690068 Return Of The Hellecasters	$19.95
00692930 Jimi Hendrix – Are You Experienced?	$19.95
00692931 Jimi Hendrix – Axis: Bold As Love	$19.95
00660192 The Jimi Hendrix – Concerts	$24.95
00692932 Jimi Hendrix – Electric Ladyland	$24.95
00690218 Jimi Hendrix – First Rays of the New Rising Sun	$24.95

00660099 Jimi Hendrix – Radio One	$24.95
00690280 Jimi Hendrix – South Saturn Delta	$19.95
00694919 Jimi Hendrix – Stone Free	$19.95
00694865 Gary Hoey – Best Of	$19.95
00660029 Buddy Holly	$19.95
00660169 John Lee Hooker – A Blues Legend	$19.95
00690054 Hootie & The Blowfish – Cracked Rear View	$19.95
00690143 Hootie & The Blowfish – Fairweather Johnson	$19.95
00694905 Howlin' Wolf	$19.95
00690136 Indigo Girls – 1200 Curfews	$22.95
00694938 Elmore James – Master Electric Slide Guitar	$19.95
00690167 Skip James Blues Guitar Collection	$16.95
00694833 Billy Joel For Guitar	$19.95
00694912 Eric Johnson – Ah Via Musicom	$19.95
00690169 Eric Johnson – Venus Isle	$22.95
00694799 Robert Johnson – At The Crossroads	$19.95
00693185 Judas Priest – Vintage Hits	$19.95
00690073 B. B. King – 1950-1957	$24.95
00690098 B. B. King – 1958-1967	$24.95
00690099 B. B. King – 1962-1971	$24.95
00690134 Freddie King Collection	$19.95
00694903 The Best Of Kiss	$24.95
00690157 Kiss – Alive	$19.95
00690163 Mark Knopfler/Chet Atkins – Neck and Neck	$19.95
00690202 Live – Secret Samadhi	$19.95
00690070 Live – Throwing Copper	$19.95
00690108 Living Colour – Best Of	$19.95
00694954 Lynyrd Skynyrd, New Best Of	$19.95
00694845 Yngwie Malmsteen – Fire And Ice	$19.95
00694956 Bob Marley – Legend	$19.95
00690239 Matchbox 20 – Yourself or Someone Like You	$19.95
00690020 Meat Loaf – Bat Out Of Hell I & II	$22.95
00690244 Megadeath – Cryptic Writings	$19.95
00690011 Megadeath – Youthanasia	$19.95
00690236 Mighty Mighty Bosstones – Let's Face It	$19.95
00690040 Steve Miller Band Greatest Hits	$19.95
00690225 Moist – Creature	$19.95
00694802 Gary Moore – Still Got The Blues	$19.95
00690103 Alanis Morissette – Jagged Little Pill	$19.95
00694958 Mountain, Best Of	$19.95
00694895 Nirvana – Bleach	$19.95
00694913 Nirvana – In Utero	$19.95
00694883 Nirvana – Nevermind	$19.95
00690026 Nirvana – Acoustic In New York	$19.95
00120112 No Doubt – Tragic Kingdom	$22.95
00690273 Oasis – Be Here Now	$19.95
00690159 Oasis – Definitely Maybe	$19.95
00690121 Oasis – (What's The Story) Morning Glory	$19.95
00690204 Offspring, The – Ixnay on the Hombre	$17.95
00690203 Offspring, The – Smash	$17.95
00694830 Ozzy Osbourne – No More Tears	$19.95
00694855 Pearl Jam – Ten	$19.95
00690053 Liz Phair – Whip Smart	$19.95
00690176 Phish – Billy Breathes	$22.95
00690240 Phish – Hoist	$19.95
00693800 Pink Floyd – Early Classics	$19.95
00694967 Police – Message In A Box Boxed Set	$70.00
00690125 Presidents of the United States of America	$19.95
00690195 Presidents of the United States of America II	$22.95
00694974 Queen – A Night At The Opera	$19.95
00694910 Rage Against The Machine	$19.95
00690145 Rage Against The Machine – Evil Empire	$19.95
00690179 Rancid – And Out Come the Wolves	$22.95

00690055 Red Hot Chili Peppers – Bloodsugarsexmagik	$19.95
00690090 Red Hot Chili Peppers – One Hot Minute	$22.95
00694892 Guitar Style Of Jerry Reed	$19.95
00694937 Jimmy Reed – Master Bluesman	$19.95
00694899 R.E.M. – Automatic For The People	$19.95
00694898 R.E.M. – Out Of Time	$19.95
00690014 Rolling Stones – Exile On Main Street	$24.95
00690186 Rolling Stones – Rock & Roll Circus	$19.95
00690135 Otis Rush Collection	$19.95
00690133 Rusted Root – When I Woke	$19.95
00690031 Santana's Greatest Hits	$19.95
00694805 Scorpions – Crazy World	$19.95
00690150 Son Seals – Bad Axe Blues	$17.95
00690128 Seven Mary Three – American Standards	$19.95
00690076 Sex Pistols – Never Mind The Bollocks	$19.95
00120105 Kenny Wayne Shepherd – Ledbetter Heights	$19.95
00690196 Silverchair – Freak Show	$19.95
00690130 Silverchair – Frogstomp	$19.95
00690041 Smithereens – Best Of	$19.95
00694885 Spin Doctors – Pocket Full Of Kryptonite	$19.95
00690124 Sponge – Rotting Pinata	$19.95
00690161 Sponge – Wax Ecstatic	$19.95
00120004 Steely Dan – Best Of	$24.95
00694921 Steppenwolf, The Best Of	$22.95
00694957 Rod Stewart – Acoustic Live	$22.95
00690021 Sting – Fields Of Gold	$19.95
00120081 Sublime	$19.95
00690242 Suede – Coming Up	$19.95
00694824 Best Of James Taylor	$16.95
00694887 Thin Lizzy – The Best Of Thin Lizzy	$19.95
00690238 Third Eye Blind	$19.95
00690022 Richard Thompson Guitar	$19.95
00690267 311	$19.95
00690030 Toad The Wet Sprocket	$19.95
00690228 Tonic – Lemon Parade	$19.95
00694411 U2 – The Joshua Tree	$19.95
00690039 Steve Vai – Alien Love Secrets	$24.95
00690172 Steve Vai – Fire Garden	$24.95
00660137 Steve Vai – Passion & Warfare	$24.95
00690023 Jimmie Vaughan – Strange Pleasures	$19.95
00660136 Stevie Ray Vaughan – In Step	$19.95
00694835 Stevie Ray Vaughan – The Sky Is Crying	$19.95
00690015 Stevie Ray Vaughan – Texas Flood	$19.95
00694776 Vaughan Brothers – Family Style	$19.95
00690217 Verve Pipe, The – Villains	$19.95
00120026 Joe Walsh – Look What I Did...	$24.95
00694789 Muddy Waters – Deep Blues	$24.95
00690071 Weezer	$19.95
00690286 Weezer – Pinkerton	$19.95
00694970 Who, The – Definitive Collection A-E	$24.95
00694971 Who, The – Definitive Collection F-Li	$24.95
00694972 Who, The – Definitive Collection Lo-R	$24.95
00694973 Who, The – Definitive Collection S-Y	$24.95